Antigone

Also available from Bloomsbury

Antigone

Slavoj Žižek

Bloomsbury Academic
An imprint of Bloomsbury Publishing Plc

BLOOMSBURY ACADEMIC
LONDON • NEW YORK • OXFORD • NEW DELHI • SYDNEY

BLOOMSBURY ACADEMIC
Bloomsbury Publishing Plc

50 Bedford Square, London, WC1B 3DP, UK
1385 Broadway, New York, NY 10018, USA
29 Earlsfort Terrace, Dublin 2, Ireland

www.bloomsbury.com

BLOOMSBURY and the Diana logo are trademarks of Bloomsbury Publishing Plc

First published 2016

© Slavoj Žižek, 2016

British Library Cataloguing-in-Publication Data
A catalogue record for this book is available from the British Library.

ISBN: PB: 9781474269377
ePDF: 9781474269384
ePub: 9781474269391

Library of Congress Cataloging-in-Publication Data
A catalog record for this book is available from the Library of Congress.

Typeset by Fakenham Prepress Solutions, Fakenham, Norfolk NR21 8NN

Contents

Foreword

Antigone – If Their Lips Weren't Sealed by Fear

Hanif Kureishi

Antigone is a particularly modern heroine. She is a rebel, a refusenik, a feminist, an anti-capitalist (principles are more important than money), a suicide perhaps, certainly a martyr, and without doubt a difficult, insistent person, not unlike some of Ibsen's women. More decisive, less irritating, talky and circular than Hamlet – but, you might say, equally teenage – she has blazed through the centuries to remain one of the great characters of all literature. Is she a saint, a criminal of extraordinary integrity, a masochist, or just stubborn and insolent? Or even 'mad', in the sense of impossible to understand?

Although psychoanalysis is not a determinism, with the parents Antigone had – the self-blinding Oedipus and the suicider Jocasta – you'd have to say she didn't have much of a chance. Nonetheless, she is splendid, a fabulous creature, vibrant in her hardness, even as she is wildly frustrating in her intransigence.

She is also a wonderful part to play for an actress. We must never forget, after all, that *Antigone* is a play, a 'noir', almost, and a profound evening's entertainment. The text, described by Hegel as 'one of the most sublime, and in every respect, most consummate works of human effort ever brought forth', is a contribution to showbiz and not a thesis, although as a character *Antigone* is infinitely interpretable and has been repeatedly written about by philosophers, psychoanalysts, feminists, literary critics and revolutionaries.

The 'anti' in the name Antigone should be emphasized. What she wants, the strong desire from which Antigone never wavers, is to bury her beloved so-called traitor brother Polyneices – lying dead and neglected outside the Palace walls – with ceremony and dignity. She is absolutely clear: he will not be carrion for dogs and vultures. She will have the rituals of mourning.

Since this is a father–daughter drama, Creon, her adversary, the man who could become her father-in-law, and who is a kind of daddy substitute, is a tough guy. Creon is a leader, a clever politician with a Mafia don side, a primal father to whom all the women must belong. He is not the sort of man to be mocked or out-thought by a young woman, one who is determined from the start not to admire him, and who is set on undermining him. As he insists, 'The laws of the city speak through me.'

Creon, then, like her own father, for whom she cared for many years, is self-blinded. There is much he cannot afford to see or acknowledge. Antigone, on the other hand, with no children to protect, can enter 'the domain of men' and attempt to persuade Creon to understand her, to recognize the absurdity of the law. She is his perfect foil and necessary nuisance, ideally placed to see on his behalf, to tease out his weaknesses and torment him.

While Antigone is betrothed to her cousin, Creon's son Haemon, Creon insists, not unreasonably, that the law, which replaces the agency of individuals, has to be obeyed. There cannot be exceptions, that is the point of the law: it is absolute. But for her the law is pathological and sadistic, and ethics are ideology. She is uninterested in happiness – she is accused by her sister Ismene of 'loving Polyneices being dead' – but the play is certainly concerned with enjoyment. If the law enjoys itself at our expense, she will also enjoy herself, perhaps too much, taking her sacrifice to its limit – death, and even beyond, into 'myth', ensuring that she will never disappear.

Antigone is certainly a feminist, a girl defying patriarchy, a lone woman standing up to a cruel man. But she ain't no sister; there's no solidarity or community in her actions. She is a rebel but not a revolutionary. She doesn't want to remove Creon and replace his dictatorship with a more democratic system. In fact Sophocles is showing us here how the law and dissent create and generate one another, illustrating the necessary tension between the state and the people, the family and the individual, man and woman.

Antigone is, in some terrible way, bound to Creon in love, as we are inevitably bound to our enemies. She is not more free than he. This couple are fascinated by one another. What is terrible about Antigone is not so much her belief, but the way she assumes it. She is entirely certain. She is no paragon; and rather than being an example of someone who sticks to their desire, she is a person who cannot think, lacking intellectual flexibility.

Her intransigence mimics that of Creon. Indeed, the two of them have similar characters, neither having any self-doubt, sceptism or ability to compromise. Both are afflicted by excessive certainty – so that the two of them will always be on a collision course. Both are shown to be monsters, and both will have to die.

This play, then, is perfectly balanced in the way it engages the audience, as it moves from argument to argument. It is a play of voices and an exercise in democracy itself, proposing no solution, but clearly displaying the most fundamental questions. There is no agreed-upon good. The good is that which can be argued about, but there is no possibility of a final position without imposing it, a form of utopia which can only lead to fascism.

Every act renders us guilty in some way. It is as if we'd like to believe we can live without hurting others. But this beautiful story of 'demonic excess' can only end badly on both sides, with Antigone killing herself and Creon having lost his son, consumed with guilt and eventually murdered by the mob, his palace burned down.

Antigone could be described as a dialectical teaching play, a 'what-if', showing human action from numerous points of view, just as the point of a psychoanalysis is not to eliminate conflicts but to expose them. The play doesn't tell us what to think, for it is not a guide to thought, but is another thing altogether: a guide to the necessity of perplexity. It illustrates a necessary conflict, showing that useful rather than deadly conflicts make democracy possible.

Introduction

Run, Antigone, Run!

The Fast Runner, a unique film retelling an old Inuit (Eskimo) legend, was made by the Canadian Inuits themselves in 2001; the director Zacharias Kunuk decided to change the ending, replacing the original slaughter in which all participants die with a more conciliatory conclusion. When a culturally sensitive journalist accused Kunuk of betraying authentic tradition for the cheap appeal to contemporary public, Kunuk replied by accusing the journalist of cultural ignorance: this very readiness to adapt the story to today's specific needs attests to the fact that the authors were still part of the ancient Inuit tradition – such 'opportunistic' rewriting is a feature of premodern cultures, while the very notion of the 'fidelity to the original' signals that we are already in the space of modernity, that we lost our immediate contact with tradition.

This is how we should approach numerous recent attempts to stage some classical opera by not only transposing its action into a different (most often contemporary) era, but also by changing some basic facts of the narrative itself. There is no a priori abstract criterion which would allow us to judge the success or failure: each such intervention is a risky act and must be judged by its own immanent standards. Such experiments often ridiculously misfire – however, not always, and there is no way to tell it in advance, so one has to take the risk. Only one thing is sure: the only way to be faithful to a classic work is to take such as risk – avoiding it, sticking to the traditional letter, is the safest way to betray the spirit of the classic. In other words, the only way to keep a classical work alive is to treat it as 'open', pointing towards the future, or, to use the metaphor evoked by Walter Benjamin, to act as if the classic work is a film for which the appropriate chemical liquid to develop it was invented only later, so that it is only today that we can get the full picture.

Among the cases of such successful changes, two stagings of Wagner's operas stand out: Jean-Pierre Ponelle's Bayreuth version of *Tristan* in which, in Act III, Tristan dies alone (Isolde stayed with her husband, King Marke, her appearance at the opera's end is merely the dying Tristan's hallucination), and Hans-Juergen Syberberg's film version of *Parsifal* (in which Amfortas' wound is a partial object, a kind of continually bleeding vagina carried on a pillow outside his body; plus, at the moment of his insight into Amfortas' suffering and rejection of Kundry, the boy who acted Parsifal is replaced by a young cold girl). In both cases, the change has a tremendous power of revelation: one cannot resist the strong impression that 'this is how it really should be'.

So can we imagine a similar change in staging *Antigone*, one of the founding narratives of the Western tradition? The path was shown by none other than Kierkegaard who, in 'The Ancient Tragical Motif as Reflected in the Modern', a chapter of Volume I of *Either/Or*, proposed his fantasy of what a modern *Antigone* would have been. The conflict is now entirely internalized: there is no longer a need for Creon. While Antigone admires and loves her father Oedipus, the public hero and savior of Thebes, she knows the truth about him (murder of the father, incestuous marriage). Her deadlock is that she is prevented from sharing this accursed knowledge (like Abraham, who also could not communicate to others the divine injunction to sacrifice his son): she cannot complain, share her pain and sorrow with others. In contrast to Sophocles' Antigone who acts (buries her brother and thus actively assumes her fate), she is unable to act, condemned forever to impassive suffering. This unbearable burden of her secret, of her destructive agalma, finally drives her to death in which only she can find peace otherwise provided by symbolizing/sharing one's pain and sorrow. And Kierkegaard's point is that this situation is no longer properly tragic (again, in a similar way that Abraham is also not a tragic figure).

We can imagine the same shift also in the case of Abraham. The God who commands Abraham to sacrifice his son is the superego-God who, for his own perverse pleasure, submits his servant to the utter test. What makes Abraham's situation non-tragic is that God's demand cannot be rendered public, shared by the community of believers, included into the big Other: the sublime tragic moment occurs precisely when the hero addresses the public with his terrible plight, when he puts into words his predicament. To put it in a succinct and unambiguous way, God's demand to Abraham has a status similar to that of a secret 'dirty' injunction of a ruler to commit a crime which the State needs, but which cannot be admitted publicly. When, in the autumn of 1586, Queen Elizabeth I was under pressure from her ministers to agree to the execution of Mary Stuart, she replied to their petition with the famous 'answer without an answer':

> If I should say I would not do what you request I might say perhaps more than I think. And if I should say I would do it, I might plunge myself into peril, whom you labour to preserve.

The message was clear: she was not ready to say that she doesn't want Mary executed, since saying this would be saying 'more than I think' – while she clearly wanted her dead, she did not want to publicly assume upon herself this act of judicial murder. The implicit message of her answer is thus a very clear one: if you are my true faithful servants, do this crime for me, kill her without making me responsible for her death, i.e. allowing me to protest my ignorance of the act and even punish some of you to sustain this false appearance ... Can we not imagine God himself giving a similar answer if Abraham were to ask him publicly, in front of his fellow wise elders, if he really wants Abraham to kill his only son? 'If I should say I do not want you to kill Isaac I might say perhaps more than I think. And if I should say you should do it, I might plunge myself into peril (of appearing an evil barbaric God, asking you to violate my own sacred Laws), from which you, my faithful follower, labour to save me.'

Furthermore, insofar as Kierkegaard's Antigone is a paradig-matically modernist figure, one should go on with his mental experiment and imagine a postmodern Antigone with, of course, a Stalinist twist to her image: in contrast to the modernist one, she should find herself in a position in which, to quote Kierkegaard himself, the ethical itself would be the temptation. One version would undoubtedly be for Antigone to publicly renounce, denounce and accuse her father (or, in a different version, her brother Polyneices) of his terrible sins out of her unconditional love for him. The Kierkegaardian catch is that such a public act would render Antigone even more isolated, absolutely alone: no one – with the exception of Oedipus himself, if he were still alive – would understand that her act of betrayal is the supreme act of love ... Is this predicament of the 'postmodern' Antigone not that of Judas, who was secretly enjoined by Christ to publicly betray him and pay the full price for it? Such a version would have been an authentic artistic event, changing our entire perception of the story.

Antigone would thus be entirely deprived of her sublime beauty – all that would signal the fact that she is not a pure and simple traitor to her father, but that she did it out of love for him, would be some barely perceptible repulsive tic, like Claudel's Sygne de Coufontaine's hysteric twitch of the lips, a tic which no longer belongs to the face: it is a grimace whose insistence disintegrates the unity of a face. Can we not imagine a similar tic of Judas – a desperate twitch of his lips signalling the terrible burden of his role?

Far from just throwing herself into death, from being possessed by a strange wish to die or to disappear, Sophocles' Antigone insists up to her death on performing a precise symbolic gesture: the proper burial of her brother. Like *Hamlet*, *Antigone* is a drama of a failed symbolic ritual – Lacan insisted on this continuity (he analysed *Hamlet* in his seminar that precedes *The Ethics of Psychoanalysis*). Antigone does not stand for some extra-symbolic real, but for the pure signifier – her 'purity' is that of a signifier. This is why, although her act is suicidal, the stakes are symbolic: her passion is death drive at its purest – but here, precisely, we should distinguish between the Freudian death drive and the Oriental nirvana. What makes Antigone a pure agent of death drive is her unconditional insistence on the demand for the symbolic ritual, an insistence which allows for no displacement or other form of compromise – this is why Lacan's formula of drive is $-D, the subject uncondi-tionally insisting on a symbolic demand.

The problem with Antigone is not the suicidal purity of her death drive but – quite the opposite – that the monstrosity of her act is covered up by its aestheticization: the moment she is excluded from the community of humans, she turns into a sublime apparition evoking our sympathy by complaining about her plight. This is one of the key dimensions of Lacan's move from Antigone to another tragic heroine, Sygne de Coufontaine from Paul Claudel's *L'otage*: there is no sublime beauty in Sygne at the play's end – all that marks her as different from common mortals is a repeated tic that momentarily disfigures her face. This feature which spoils the harmony of her beautiful face, the detail that sticks out and makes it ugly, is the material trace of her resistance to being co-opted into the universe of symbolic debt and guilt. And, back to Christ, this, then, should be the first step of a consequent reading of Christianity: the dying Christ is on the side of Sygne, not on the side of Antigone; Christ on the cross is not a sublime apparition but an embarrassing monstrosity. Another aspect of this monstrosity was clearly perceived by Rembrandt, whose 'Lazarus', one of the most traumatic classic paintings, is a depiction of Christ at the moment he is raising Lazarus from the dead. What strikes the eye is not only the figure of Lazarus, a monstrous living dead returning to life, but, even more so, the terrified expression on Christ's face, as if he is a magician shocked that his spell really worked, disgusted by what he brought back to life, aware that he is playing with forces better left alone. This is a true Kierkegaardian Christ, shocked not by his mortality but by the heavy burden of his supernatural powers which border on blasphemy, the blasphemy at work in every good biography: 'Biography is in fact one of the occult arts. It uses scientific means – documentation, analysis, inquiry – to achieve a hermetic end: the transformation of base material into gold. Its final intention is the most ambitious and blasphemous of all – to bring back a human being to life.'

Antigone is thus to be opposed to Claudel's Sygne de Coufontaine: if Oedipus and Antigone are the exemplary cases of Ancient tragedy, Sygne stands for the Christian tragedy. Sygne lives in the modern world where God is dead: there is no objective Fate, our fate is our own choice, we are fully responsible for it. Sygne first follows the path of ecstatic love to the end, sacrificing her good, her ethical substance, for God, for His pure Otherness; and she doesn't do it on account of some external pressure, but out of the innermost freedom of her being – she cannot blame any Fate when she finds herself totally humiliated, deprived of all ethical substance of her being. This, however, is why Sygne's tragedy is much more radical than that of Oedipus or Antigone: when, mortally wounded after receiving the bullet meant for her despicable and hated husband, she refuses to confer any deeper sacrificial meaning on her suicidal interposition, there is no tragic beauty in this refusal – her 'NO' is signalled by a mere repellent grimace, a compulsive tic of her face. There is no tragic beauty because her utter sacrifice deprived her of all inner beauty and ethical grandeur – they all went into it, so that she remains a disgusting excremental stain of humanity, a living shell deprived of life. There is no love here either; all her love went into her previous renunciations. In a way, Sygne is here crucified, her 'NO' like Christ's 'Father, why did you abandon me?' – which is also a gesture of defiance, of 'Up yours!' directed at the God-Father. Balmes is right to point out that this properly Christian 'NO' in all its forms is the 'unthinkable' traumatic core of pure love, a scandal which undermines it from within. Here is his breathtakingly precise formulation:

> The unthinkable in pure love is, in a sense, Christianity
> itself, the scandal of the Cross, the Passion and the death
> of Christ, the 'Why did you abandon me?' from the psalm
> taken over by Christ and to which the mystics of pure love
> conferred a radicality intolerable for the Church.

This moment of tragedy, this return of the tragic in the very heart of Christianity as the religion of love, is also the point which the self-erasing mystique of ecstatic love cannot properly grasp: when mystics talk about the 'Night of the World', they directly identify this Night (the withdrawal from external reality into the void of pure innerness) with the divine Beatitude, with the self-erasing immersion into Divinity; for Christianity, in contrast, the unbearable and unsurpassable tension remains, there is an ex-timate 'NO' in the very heart of the loving YES to it all. This 'NO' has nothing to do with the imaginary logic of hainamoration, of the reversal of narcissistic love into hatred.

Claudel himself found Sygne's refusal of reconciliation with Turelure at the end of *L'otage* mysterious: it imposed itself on him while he was writing the drama, since it was not part of the original plan (first, he intended the marriage of Sygne and Turelure to mark the reconciliation of the ancien regime and the new regime in the Restoration; then, he planned Badillon to convince the dying Sygne to give the demanded sign of pardon and reconciliation to Turelure). Significantly, most of the critics perceived Sygne's refusal not as the mark of her radicality, but as the mark of her failure to follow through with the sacrifice demanded from her, i.e. to consent fully to the marriage with the despicable Turelure. The idea is that, by way of refusing a sign of consent and dying in ice-cold silence and withdrawal, Sygne disavows religious principles which hitherto dictated her behaviour – as Abel Hermant wrote:

> Turelure tries to extract from Sygne a word, a sign of pardon, which would be for him the sign that he has definitely conquered her and reached the end of his ambitions. But Sygne refuses this pardon, on which nonetheless her eternal salvation seems to depend. She thus renders all her sacrifices worthless in the last minute.

To such readings, Claudel feebly protested: 'I believe she is saved', conceding that the meaning of her final act is not clear to him:

> At the play's end, the persons escape all psychological investigation: at the human level, Sygne of course refused to fulfil her sacrifice; we do not know more about it, and the author himself can only 'suppose' a meaning to her final gesture.

However, in order to locate a figure which clearly opposes Antigone, we do not have to reach forward to European modernity – we find it already in the Ancient Greek universe: Electra. In both cases we have a feminine couple, with a sister (Ismene, Chrysothemis) who is more human, full of empathy but also of pragmatic conformism. In Sophocles' Electra, both Orestes and Electra are living dead (like Antigone after her banishment from the city) – recall Orestes saying to Aegisthus: 'Don't you realize yet / that you're talking to dead men alive?' Chorus tried to bring Electra back to ordinary reality: 'Yet you run yourself out / in a grief with no cure, / no time-limit, no measure. / It is a knot no one can untie. / Why are you so in love with / things unbearable.' Like Antigone, Electra reasserts her total commitment – but, unlike Antigone, she endorses it in all its violence: 'By dread things I am compelled. I know that. / I see the trap closing. / I know what I am. / But while life is in me / I will not stop this violence. No.' And she is well aware that this violence slips over into madness: 'I ask one thing: let me go mad in my own way.'

With regard to this violence, consider the final confrontation between Orestes and Aegisthus, who also declares: 'I'm a dead man. No way out. / But let me just say –' Immediately he is interrupted by Electra addressing Orestes: 'No! / Don't let him speak – […] Kill him at once. / Throw his corpse out / for scavengers to get.' (So, exactly like Polyneices in Antigone, he should not be properly buried.) Orestes obeys his sister's injunction and orders Aegisthus to enter the house, to which Aegisthus first retorts: 'Why take me inside? / If the deed is honourable, what need of darkness?' But then he immediately concedes: 'You lead the way.' Orestes: 'No you go first.' Aegisthus: 'Afraid I'll escape?' Orestes: 'You shall not die on your own terms.' Chorus's final lines then render Orestes' cruel act in a surprising empty gesture of celebration: 'You took aim and struck; you have won your way through / to the finish.' This finale is an effective anti-Antigone: no ritual, no speech, just a killing performed in darkness, like a mob liquidation. (In my version, I also tried to imagine an act of liquidation, but an act which, instead of being performed in secret, publicly declares itself.)

What all these dark echoes of figures like Antigone and Electra indicate is the obscure and hidden obverse of the Ancient Greek universe, the limit of the farmonious order deployed by Solon, the founder of the Athenian democracy, in his famous ethico-political poem on eunomia – the beautiful order:

These things my spirit bids me
teach the men of Athens:
that Dysnomia
brings countless evils for the city,
but Eunomia brings order
and makes everything proper,
by enfolding the unjust in fetters,
smoothing those things that are rough,
stopping greed,
sentencing hybris to obscurity
making the flowers of mischief to wither,
and straightening crooked judgments.
It calms the deeds of arrogance

and stops the bilious anger of harsh strife.
Under its control, all things are proper
and prudence reigns human affairs.

No wonder the same principle is asserted in the famous chorus on the uncanny/demonic dimension of man from Sophocles' *Antigone*:

If man honours the laws of the land, and reveres the Gods of the State, proudly his city shall stand; but a cityless outcast I rate who so bold in his pride from the path of right does depart; never may I sit by his side, or share the thoughts of his heart.

(Some even propose a much more radical translation of the last line, like A. Oksenberg Rorty: 'a person without a city, beyond human boundary, a horror, a pollution to be avoided.') One should recall here that this chorus reacts to the news that someone (at this point one doesn't yet know who) violated Creon's prohibition and performed funeral rites on Polyneices' body – it is Antigone herself who is implicitly castigated as the 'cityless outcast' engaged in excessive demonic acts which disturb the eumonia of the state, fully reasserted in the last lines of the play:

The most important part of happiness
is therefore wisdom — not to act impiously
towards the gods, for boasts of arrogant men
bring on great blows of punishment
so in old age men can discover wisdom.

From the standpoint of eumonia, Antigone is definitely demonic/uncanny: her defying act expresses a stance of de-measured excessive insistence which disturbs the 'beautiful order' of the city; her unconditional ethics violates the harmony of the polis and is as such 'beyond human boundary'. The irony is that, while Antigone presents herself as the guardian of the immemorial laws which sustain human order, she acts as a freakish and ruthless abomination; there definitely is something cold and monstrous about her, as is rendered by the contrast between her and her warmly human sister Ismene. This uncanny dimension is signalled by the ambiguity in the name 'Antigone': it can be read as 'unbending', coming from 'anti-' and '-gon/-gony' (corner, bend, angle), but also as 'opposed to motherhood' or 'in place of a mother' from the root 'gone', 'that which generates' ('gonos', '-gony', as in 'theogony'). It is difficult to resist the temptation of positing a link between the two meanings: is being-a-mother not the basic form of a woman's 'bending', subordination, so that Antigone's uncompromising attitude has to entail the rejection of motherhood? Ironically, in the original myth (reported by Hyginus in his Fabulae 72), Antigone was a mother: when she was caught in the act of performing funeral rites for her brother Polyneices, Creon handed her over for execution to his son Haemon, to whom she had been betrothed. But Haemon, while he pretended to put her to death, smuggled her out of the way, married her, and had a son by her. In time the son grew up and came to Thebes, where Creon detected him by the bodily mark which all descendants of the Sparti or Dragon-men bore on their bodies. Creon was inexorable; so Haemon killed himself and his wife Antigone ... (There are indications that Hyginus here followed Euripides, who also wrote a tragedy *Antigone*, of which a few fragments survived, and one of them is: 'Man's best possession is a sympathetic wife' – definitely not Sophocles' *Antigone*.) If we were to tell this story to someone not knowing about the origins of the Antigone story, he would probably dismiss Hyginus's version as a kitsch melodrama.

So while Antigone is an uncanny figure who disturbs the harmony of the traditional universe, one should no less resist the opposite temptation to interpret her as a proto-modern emancipatory heroine who speaks for all those excluded from the public domain, all those whose voices are not heard; in short, for what Agamben calls *homo sacer*. Agamben's analysis should be given its full radical character: his notion of *homo sacer* should NOT be watered down into an element of a radical-democratic project whose aim is to renegotiate or redefine the limits of in- and exclusion, so that the symbolic field will be more and more open also to the voices of those who are excluded by the hegemonic configuration of the public discourse. Therein resides the gist of Judith Butler's reading of *Antigone*:

the limit for which she stands, a limit for which no standing, no translatable representation is possible, is [...] the trace of

an alternate legality that haunts the conscious, public sphere
as its scandalous future.

Antigone formulates her claim on behalf of all those who, like the
sans-papiers in today's France, are without a full and definite socio-
ontological status, and Butler herself refers here to Agamben's
homo sacer. Which is why one should pin down neither the
position from which (on behalf of which) Antigone is speaking,
nor the object of her claim: in spite of her emphasis of the unique
position of the brother, this object is not as unambiguous as it
may appear (is Oedipus himself also not her (half)brother?);
her position is not simply feminine, because she enters the male
domain of public affairs – in addressing Creon, the head of state,
she speaks like him, appropriating his authority in a perverse/
displaced way; and neither does she speak on behalf of kinship,
as Hegel claimed, since her very family stands for the ultimate
(incestuous) corruption of the proper order of kinship. Her claim
thus displaces the fundamental contours of the Law, what the Law
excludes and includes.

   Butler develops her reading in contrast to two main opponents,
not only Hegel but also Lacan. In Hegel, the conflict is conceived
as internal to the socio-symbolic order, as the tragic split of the
ethical substance: Creon and Antigone stand for its two compo-
nents, state and family, Day and Night, the human legal order and
the divine subterranean order. Lacan, on the contrary, emphasizes
how Antigone, far from standing for kinship, assumes the limit-
position of the very instituting gesture of the symbolic order, of the
impossible zero-level of symbolization, which is why she stands
for death drive: while still alive, she is already dead with regard to
the symbolic order, excluded from the socio-symbolic coordinates.
In what one is almost tempted to call a dialectical synthesis, Butler
rejects both extremes (Hegel's location of the conflict WITHIN the
socio-symbolic order; Lacan's notion of Antigone as standing for
the going-to-the-limit, for reaching the OUTSIDE of this order):
Antigone undermines the existing symbolic order not simply from
its radical outside, but from a utopian standpoint of aiming at its
radical rearticulation. Antigone is a 'living dead' not in the sense
(which Butler attributes to Lacan) of entering the mysterious

domain of Até,[1] of going to the limit of the Law; she is a 'living dead' in the sense of publicly assuming an uninhabitable position, a position for which there is no place in the public space – not a priori, but only with regard to the way this space is structured now, in the historically contingent and specific conditions.

This, then, is Butler's central point against Lacan: Lacan's very radicality (the notion that Antigone locates herself in the suicidal outside of the symbolic order) reasserts this order, the order of the established kinship relations, silently assuming that the ultimate alternative is the one between the symbolic Law of (fixed patriarchal) kinship relations and its suicidal ecstatic transgression. What about the third option: that of rearticulating these kinship relations themselves, i.e. of reconsidering the symbolic Law as the set of contingent social arrangements open to change? Antigone speaks for all the subversive 'pathological' claims which crave to be admitted into the public space; however, to identify what she stands for in this reading with *homo sacer* misses the basic thrust of Agamben's analysis. There is no place in Agamben for the 'democratic' project of 'renegotiating' the limit which separates full citizens from *homo sacer* by gradually allowing their voices to be heard; his point is, rather, that, in today's 'post-politics', the very democratic public space is a mask concealing the fact that, ultimately, we are all *homo sacer*. Does, then, this mean that Agamben fully and simply participates in the line of those who, like Adorno and Foucault, identify as the secret telos of the development of our societies a total closure of the 'administered world' in which we are all reduced to the status of objects of 'biopolitics'? Although Agamben denies any 'democratic' way out, in his detailed reading of Saint Paul, he violently reasserts the 'revolutionary' Messianic dimension – and if this Messianic dimension means anything at all, it means that 'mere life' is no longer the ultimate terrain of politics. That is to say, what is suspended in the Messianic attitude

---

[1] *Até* – the Ancient Greek goddess of misfortune, madness and ruin; it can also be used to designate the action that a hero performs because of his/her hubris and that ends in his/her downfall, as well as the prohibited domain that the hero enters when s/he performs such an act.

of 'awaiting the end of time' is precisely the central place of 'mere life'; in clear contrast to it, the fundamental feature of post-politics is the reduction of politics to 'biopolitics' in the precise sense of administering and regulating 'mere life'.

Which Antigone would fit this contemporary condition? Coping with this problem, I imagined another triad: the starting point remains the same, and it is only at the crucial point in the middle of the play – the big confrontation between Antigone and Creon – that the three versions would diverge:

- The first version follows Sophocles' denouement, and the concluding chorus praises Antigone's unconditional insistence on her principle – *fiat justitia pereat mundus* …

- The second version shows what would have happened if Antigone were to win, convincing Creon to allow the proper burial of Polyneices, i.e. if her principled attitude were to prevail. In this version, the concluding chorus sings a Brechtian praise of pragmatism: the ruling class can afford to obey honour and rigid principles, while ordinary people pay the price for it.

- In the third version, Chorus is no longer the purveyor of stupid commonplace wisdoms, it becomes an active agent. At the climactic moment of the ferocious debate between Antigone and Creon, Chorus steps forward, castigating both of them for their stupid conflict which threatens the survival of the entire city. Acting like a kind of *comité de salut public*, Chorus takes over as a collective organ and imposes a new rule of law, installing people's democracy in Thebes. Creon is deposed, both Creon and Antigone are arrested, put to trial, swiftly condemned to death and liquidated.

Sophocles' *Antigone* is thus retold here in the mode of Bertolt Brecht's three learning plays (*Jasager, Neinsager, Jasager 2*): at the crucial point of decision, events take three different directions – a procedure later used in two films, Krzystof Kieslowski's *Blind Chance* and Tom Tykwer's *Run, Lola, Run*. My premise is that such a staging confronts us with a true *Antigone* for our times, ruthlessly abandoning our sympathy and compassion for the play's heroine, making her part of the problem, and proposing a way out which shatters us in our humanitarian complacency.

My retelling is consciously anachronistic – suffice it to mention Kol Nidre to which the Chorus refers, although it appeared only in the second half of the first millennium of our era. Relying on Ian Johnston's translation of Sophocles, the text freely borrows ideas and formulations from Talmud, Euripides' *Electra*, Hegel's *Phenomenology of Spirit*, Walter Benjamin's essay on the art of translation, Brecht's poems, Orson Welles's *Citizen Kane*, Paul Claudel's *Hostage*, Panait Istrati, Vladimir Safatle, Alenka Zupancic, etc. etc. It doesn't pretend to be a work of art but an ethico-political exercise.

The Three Lives of Antigone

Chorus Leader

A lean rock stands proudly alone in deep grass.
But when strong man's hands raise it, worms, insects,
roaches, all the swarming and disgusting murmur of life
confronts the eye, a chaos even gods can't master.
Such is our ultimate reality. Some heroic men
attempt to introduce some harmony and order
into this chaos, but they miserably fail, their acts
only destabilizing further the cosmic order.
Our life's a broken vessel, its fragments scattered.
It's as if gods are playing dice with us –
when a life story is told, we note how at many points
it may have taken another turn. While there's no way
to bring the fragments together and restore the vessel
in its harmony, we can do another thing. We can tell
a hero's life so that, at the point of bifurcation
when gods threw their dice, we narrate
all possible throws of the dice. In this way,
we get many stories in parallel, one over the other,
and while they do not form a harmonious Whole,
they do confront us with a complete picture.
From it we learn how things might have taken
a much better turn, but sometimes also how
what appears to us a bad turn was luck in disguise
since other turns would have been much worse.
Such is the case with poor Antigone who wanted to see
her treasonous brother, killed in the onslaught
on his own city of Thebes, properly buried.
Our story begins in front of the royal palace …

[*In Thebes, directly in front of the royal palace, which stands
in the background, its main doors facing the audience. Enter*
Antigone *leading* **Ismene** *away from the palace*]

Ismene

Why did you bring me here, outside the gates?
You're thinking of some dark and gloomy news.

Antigone

Look – what's Creon doing with our two brothers?
He's honouring one with a full funeral
and treating the other one disgracefully!
Eteocles, they say, has had his burial
according to our customary rites,
to win him honour with the dead below.

But as for Polyneices, who perished
so miserably, an order has gone out
throughout the city – that's what people say.
He's to have no funeral or lament,
but to be left unburied and unwept,
a sweet treasure for the birds to look at,
for them to feed on to their heart's content.

Anyone who acts against the order
will be stoned to death before the city.

Ismene

Oh my poor sister, if that's what's happening,
what can I say that would be any help
to ease the situation or resolve it?

Antigone

Think whether you will work with me in this
and act together. Will you help these hands
take up Polyneices' corpse and bury it?

Ismene

Your love for your brother is so strange,
I do not recognize myself in it. There's no compassion
in it, no warm feeling for the beloved.
It is as if you love him to be dead,
as if you're ready to destroy what you love.

Antigone

True love is cold, more cold than death itself.
It's not a matter of feeling which sways here and there.
Firm as a rock, it brushes off the sway of emotions,
easily enduring all pressure and constraint.

Ismene
A woman should not talk like that, not ever.
We must remember that by birth we're women,
and, as such, we shouldn't fight with men.
Since those who rule are much more powerful,
we must obey in this and in events
which bring us even harsher agonies.
So I'll ask those underground for pardon –
since I'm being compelled, I will obey
those in control. That's what I'm forced to do.
It makes no sense to try to do too much.

Antigone
Well, if you wish, you can show contempt
for those laws the gods all hold in honour.

Ismene
I'm not disrespecting them. But I can't act
against the state. That's not in my nature.

Antigone
Let nature then be your excuse. Just don't forget
you chose it. My choice is different, so I'm going now
to make a burial mound for my dear brother.

Ismene (*whispers to herself*)
You've also made a choice. Your duty's your excuse.

[*Exit* **Antigone** *away from the palace.* **Ismene** *watches her go and then returns slowly into the palace. Enter the* **Chorus of Theban elders** *with* **Creon**]

Creon
I have the throne, all royal power,
for I'm the one most closely linked by blood
to those who have been killed. Let Zeus know,
the god who always watches everything,
I would not stay silent if I saw disaster
moving here against the citizens,
a threat to their security. That's why

I've announced to all citizens
my orders for the sons of Oedipus.
Eteocles, who perished in the fight
to save our city, the best and bravest
of our spearmen, will have his burial,
with all those purifying rituals
which accompany the noblest corpses,
as they move below. As for his brother –
that Polyneices, who returned from exile,
eager to wipe out in all-consuming fire
his ancestral city and its native gods,
keen to seize upon his family's blood
and lead men into slavery – for him,
the proclamation in the state declares
he'll have no burial mound, no funeral rites,
and no lament. He'll be left unburied,
his body there for birds and dogs to eat,
a clear reminder of his shameful fate.
That's my decision. And if anyone thinks
of contravening it, just imagine the consequences.
If Polyneices is given a proper burial,
the people of our city will react with fury
against such an act of honouring the traitor,
there will be blood, and the whole city of Thebes
will become a funeral pyre for Polyneices.
I thus beseech you: do not yield to those
who contravene my orders. Their sense of justice
is misplaced, it is the deceiving mask
of a desire for death and destruction.
Even if they appear to perform a sacred rite, their god
is none other than Bacchus who wants to drag us all
into the dark abyss of the orgy of destruction.
So learn to recognize beneath the noble face
of a mourner the crazy drunken head of Bacchus.

Chorus Leader
No one is such a fool that he loves death.

[*Enter a* **guard**, *coming towards the palace*]

Creon

What's happening that's made you so upset?
Clearly you have news of something ominous.

Guard

It's about Polyneices' corpse.
Someone has buried it and disappeared,
after spreading thirsty dust onto the flesh
and undertaking all appropriate rites.

Creon

What are you saying? What man would dare this?

Guard

I don't know. Whoever did it left no trace.
The corpse was hidden, but not in a tomb.
It was lightly covered up with dirt,
as if someone wanted to avert a curse.

Chorus Leader

My lord, I've been wondering for some time now –
could this act not be something from the gods?

Creon

Stop now – before what you're about to say
enrages me completely and reveals
that you're not only old but stupid, too.
No one can tolerate what you've just said,
when you claim gods might care about this corpse.

[*Enter the* **Guard***, bringing* **Antigone** *with him. She is not resisting*]

Guard

This here's the one who carried out the act.
This girl here – we saw her giving that dead man's corpse
full burial rites. When seeing a naked corpse, she uttered
a distressing painful cry, just like a bird
who's seen an empty nest, its fledglings gone.
She screamed out a lament, then right away her hands
threw on the thirsty dust. She lifted up
a finely made bronze jug and then three times

poured out her tributes to the dead.
When we saw that, we rushed up right away
and grabbed her. She was not afraid at all.
We charged her with her previous offence
as well as this one. She just kept standing there,
denying nothing.

Creon

            You there – you with your face
bent down towards the ground, what do you say?
Do you deny you did this or admit it?

Antigone

I admit I did it. I won't deny that.

Creon

Were you aware there was a proclamation
forbidding what you did?

Antigone

             I'd heard of it.
How could I not? It was public knowledge.

Creon

And yet you dared to break those very laws?

Antigone

Yes. Nothing that you proclaimed is strong enough
to let a mortal override the gods
and their unwritten and unchanging laws.
They're not just for today or yesterday,
but exist forever, and no one knows
where they first appeared. So I did not mean
to let a fear of any human will
lead to my punishment among the gods.
I know all too well I'm going to die –
how could I not? – it makes no difference
what you decree.

Creon

These laws of yours – I don't know

what you are talking about, you insolent girl.
I deal with what I see, our city, its written laws
that people know and have to obey. Your laws,
I do not see them.

Antigone
My immemorial laws –
you have to believe in them to see them.

Creon
I see – so they are fits of your imagination?

Antigone
Once you believe in them, you see that they are real,
much more real than what you see, much more inviolable,
although you cannot touch them.

Chorus Leader
It's clear enough
the spirit in this girl is passionate –
her father was the same. She has no sense
of compromise in times of trouble. What's wrong with her,
is indicated by her name. It means 'unbending',
but also 'against generating'. Being a mother
is how women in our society bend and subordinate
to man's superior will by giving birth. So we were wrong
and she's a fool who loves death. Crazy and insolent,
by far not as modest as she claims to be.
If she wanted just to be faithful to her gods
of underground, she should celebrate them underground,
hidden out of public sight, in the family haven.
By stepping out and speaking in public about them,
confronting the king, she entered the domain of men.
Her words may sound feminine, but her act was manly.

Creon (*to the* **Chorus Leader**)
This girl here was already very insolent
in contravening laws we had proclaimed.
Here she again displays her proud contempt –
having done the act, she now boasts of it.
She laughs at what she's done. Well, in this case,

if she gets her way and goes unpunished,
then she's the man here, not me.

Antigone
Take me and kill me – what more do you want?

Creon
Me? Nothing. In all this I'm for nothing. When I speak,
the laws of our city speak through me. I am just a mediator,
a medium through which justice reaches its target.
With that, as nothing, I have everything.

Antigone
Then why delay? But where could I gain greater glory
than setting my own brother in his grave?
All those here would confirm this pleases them
if their lips weren't sealed by fear – being king,
which offers all sorts of various benefits,
means you can talk and act just as you wish.

Creon
In all of Thebes, you're the only one
who looks at things that way.

Antigone
                    They share my views,
but they keep their mouths shut just for you.

Creon
These views of yours – so different from the rest –
don't they bring you any sense of shame?

Antigone
No – there's nothing shameful in honouring
my mother's children.

Creon
                    Do not make it too easy for yourself,
you insolent kid. Your brother was a traitor to his city,
because of his vile acts many widows are shedding tears
every night. He was destroying this country,
while your other brother went to his death defending it.

Antigone
In the world below such actions are perhaps no crime.

Creon
Who knows what rules hold down there, in that place
from which no one has yet returned back to life.
If things stand like you say, then the world below
is a strange place were justice counts for nothing.
Methinks that in a just world, an enemy
can never be a friend, not even in death. When one dies,
our deeds are measured with the impartial eyes of gods,
and one is allocated a proper place in the scale of justice.
Even if, while alive, a vile man may succeed
in deceiving others and was hailed as hero, after his death
his deeds appear as what they were and he is hated.

Antigone
But my nature is to love. I cannot hate.

Creon
Sometimes one's nature is a bad guide. I also do not hate
your brother – how could I, I am his uncle. It's not hatred
but justice which speaks through my acts and decisions.
So go down to the dead. If you must love, love them.
No woman's going to defy me in the public space
and govern me – no, no – not while I'm still alive.

[*Enter two* **attendants** *from the house bringing* **Ismene** *to* **Creon**]

Creon
You there – do you admit you played your part
in this burial, or will you swear an oath
you had no knowledge of it?

Ismene
                I did it –
so I bear the guilt as well.

Antigone
                No, no –
justice will not allow you to say that.
You didn't want to. I didn't work with you.

Ismene
But now you're in trouble, I'm not ashamed
of suffering, too, as your companion.
Let me respect the dead and die with you.

Antigone
Don't try to share my death or make a claim
to actions which you did not do. I'll die –
and that will be enough.

Ismene
                    I feel so wretched leaving you to die.

Antigone
But you chose life – it was my choice to die.
Be brave. You're alive. But my spirit died
some time ago so I might help the dead.

Ismene
How could I live alone, without you here?

Creon
Don't speak of her being here. Her life is over.

Ismene
You're going to kill your own son's bride?

Creon
Why not? There are other fields for him to plough.

Ismene (*silently to herself*)
Our unfortunate father was ploughing his own mother's field.

Chorus Leader
So she must die – that seems decided on.

Creon
Yes – for you and me the matter's closed.

[**Creon** *leaves the scene*]

Antigone
In my wretchedness I have no home,
not with human beings or corpses,

not with the living or the dead.
A hero is alive while dead, he goes on living
in the glorious memory of his countrymen, while I am dead
while still alive, an abject and embarrassment
to people's eyes. So who am I?
I've heard about a guest of ours,
daughter of Tantalus, from Phrygia –
she went to an excruciating death
in Sipylus, right on the mountain peak.
The stone there, just like clinging ivy,
wore her down, and now, so people say,
the snow and rain never leave her there,
as she laments. Below her weeping eyes
her neck is wet with tears. God brings me
to a final rest which most resembles hers.

Chorus
It's a fine thing for a woman,
once she's dead, to have it said she shared,
in life and death, the fate of demi-gods.
But you, Antigone, you're not yet dead –
and while still alive, you already weave a myth
about yourself, imagining how you will look when dead.
When you talk like that, no tears can be shed,
only a smile can pass our lips – a smile at a girl
in love with herself, vain enough to think
about her look even when she is about to die.
Yes, you sacrificed everything, but you did not sacrifice
your sacrifice itself. You gave away everything,
but you did not give away your act of giving itself.
It's only when you do that, when you not only disappear,
but when your very act of disappearing disappears,
that you are no longer in love with yourself,
with your noble gesture, and reach true modesty.

Antigone
Oh, you are mocking me! Why do you
insult me now right to my face,
without waiting for my death?

In my wretchedness I have no home,
not with human beings or corpses,
not with the living or the dead.
This is my reward for covering my brother's corpse.
However, for wise people I was right
to honour you. I'd never have done it
for children of my own, not as their mother,
nor for a dead husband lying in decay –
no, not in defiance of the citizens.
What law do I appeal to, claiming this?
If my husband died, there'd be another one,
and if I were to lose a child of mine
I'd have another with some other man.
But since my father and my mother, too,
are hidden away in Hades' house,
I'll never have another living brother.
That was the law I used to honour you.

Chorus
Your words tell more truth than the thoughts behind them.
Now we see that the law you honour
is just about you and your brother,
not about respect for all who die.
It's about a girl deprived of her last toy.

[*The* **attendants** *take* **Antigone** *away for execution. Enter*
Haemon *from the palace*]

Creon
My son, have you heard the sentence that's been passed
upon your bride? And have you now come here
angry at your father? Or are you loyal to me,
on my side no matter what I do?

Haemon
Father, I'm yours. For me your judgements
and the ways you act on them are good –
I shall follow them.

Creon
                            Indeed, my son,
that's how your heart should always be resolved,
to stand behind your father's judgement.
So spit this girl out – she's your enemy.
Let her marry someone else in Hades.
Anyone who's proud and violates our laws
or thinks he'll tell our leaders what to do,
wins no praise from me. No. We must obey
whatever man the city puts in charge,
no matter what the issue – great or small,
just or unjust. For there's no greater evil
than a lack of leadership. That destroys
whole cities, turns households into ruins,
and in war makes soldiers break and run away.
When men succeed, what keeps their lives secure
in almost every case is their obedience.
That's why they must support those in control,
and never let some woman beat us down.
If we must fall from power, let that come
at some man's hand – at least, we won't be called
inferior to any woman.

Chorus
Unless we're being deceived by our old age,
what you've just said seems reasonable to us.

Haemon
Your words are right, but others might be good as well.
Your gaze makes citizens afraid – they can't
say anything you would not like to hear.
But in the darkness I can hear them talk –
the city is upset about the girl.
They say of all women here she least deserves
the worst of deaths for her most glorious act.
When in the slaughter her own brother died,
she did not just leave him there unburied,
to be ripped apart by carrion dogs or birds.
Surely she deserves some golden honour?

That's the dark secret rumour people speak.
For me, father, nothing is more valuable
than your well-being. For any children,
what could be a greater honour to them
than their father's thriving reputation?
So don't let your mind dwell on just one thought,
that what you say is right and nothing else.
A man who thinks that only he is wise,
that he can speak and think like no one else,
when such men are exposed, then all can see
their emptiness inside. For any man,
even if he's wise, there's nothing shameful
in learning many things, staying flexible.
So end your anger. Permit yourself to change.
For if I, as a younger man, may state
my views, I'd say it would be for the best
if men by nature understood all things –
if not, and that is usually the case,
when men speak well, it good to learn from them.

Creon (*whispers to himself*)
Yes, men may murmur and complain about my deeds,
but they still want it done – by someone else,
just not by them. I acted here as a true leader –
in doing what I did, I effectively enacted
what people are afraid to admit that they want.
People are hypocrites, they want a dirty deed done
and they want to keep their hands clean.

Chorus Leader
The things which you both said were excellent.
My lord, if what your son has said is relevant
it seems appropriate to learn from him,
and you too, Haemon, listen to the king.

Creon
And men my age – are we then going to school
to learn what's wise from men as young as him?

Haemon

There's nothing wrong in that. And if I'm young,
don't think about my age – look at what I do.

Creon

And what you do – does that include this,
honouring those who act against our laws?

Haemon

What do you want – to speak and never hear someone reply?

[*Exit* **Haemon**, *running back into the palace. Enter* **Teiresias**, *led by a young boy*]

Creon

What brought you here, old Teiresias? It must be
the dark clouds that are gathering above our Thebes …

Teiresias

… not just dark clouds – can't you see how it already rains,
and how the torrent will wash our noble city away?
It's all your fault. You do know how to argue,
you've got a quick tongue and seem intelligent,
but your words don't make any sense at all. You unhappy man,
you've no idea just what it is you were saying
when you prohibited Polyneices' funeral rites.
You've gone mad! It is not Antigone who is possessed
by demonic madness, it is you, our king.

Creon

These are harsh words
from an old wise man. Can you justify them?

Teiresias

What makes you mad is your very reasoning.
It ignores ancient traditions. You act as if you do not live among us,
people rooted in traditions from times immemorial.
To the gods we mortals are all ignorant.
Those old traditions from our ancestors, the ones
We've had as long as time itself,
no argument will ever overthrow, in spite of subtleties

sharp minds invent. So when you oppose the madness of Bacchus,
you display a madness of your own.

Creon

No subtle sophistry
dwells in my words. All that I did was based
on sane and wise consideration. My only purpose was
to save our city-state from chaos and destruction.

Teiresias
You may think you're sane, but it was your sane reasoning
which made our state sick – your policies have done this.
In the city our altars and our hearths have been defiled
all of them, with rotting flesh brought there
by birds and dogs from Oedipus's son,
who lies there miserably dead. The gods
no longer will accept our sacrifice,
our prayers, our thigh bones burned in fire.
No bird will shriek out a clear sign to us,
for they have gorged themselves on fat and blood
from a man who's dead. Consider this, my son.
All men make mistakes – that's not uncommon.
But when they do, they're no longer foolish
or subject to bad luck if they try to fix
the evil into which they've fallen,
once they give up their intransigence.
Make concessions to the dead – what's the glory
in killing a dead person one more time?
In doing so, you will not see
the sun race through its cycle many times
before you lose a child of your own loins,
a corpse in payment for these corpses.
You've thrown down to those below someone
from up above – in your arrogance
you've moved a living soul into a grave,
leaving here a body owned by gods below –
unburied, dispossessed, unsanctified.
That's no concern of yours or gods above.
In this you violate the ones below.

[*Exit* **Teiresias***, led by the young boy*]

Chorus Leader
My lord, my lord, such dreadful prophecies –
you need to listen to some good advice.

Creon (*visibly shaken*)
Tell me what to do. Speak up. I'll do it.

Chorus Leader
Go and release the girl from her rock tomb.

Then prepare a grave for that unburied corpse.

Go now and get this done. Don't give the work
to other men to do.

Creon
                        I'll go just as I am.
Come, you servants, each and every one of you.
Come on. Bring axes with you. Go there quickly –
up to the higher ground. I've changed my mind.

[**Creon** *and his* **attendants** *hurry offstage*]

Chorus
There are many uncanny and demonic things,
but nothing more uncanny and demonic than man.
He's taught himself speech and wind-swift thought,
trained his feelings for communal civic life,
learning to escape the icy shafts of frost,
volleys of pelting rain in winter storms,
the harsh life lived under the open sky.
That's man – so resourceful in all he does.
There's no event his skill cannot confront –
other than death – that alone he cannot shun.
The qualities of his inventive skills
bring arts beyond his dreams and lead him on,
sometimes to evil and sometimes to good.
If he treats his country's laws with due respect
and honours justice by swearing on the gods,
he wins high honours in his city.
But when he grows bold and turns to evil,

then he has no city. A man like that –
let him not share my home or know my mind.
The most important part of true success
is therefore wisdom – not to act impiously
towards the gods, for boasts of arrogant men
bring on great blows of punishment –
so in old age men can discover wisdom.

[*Enter a* **Messenger**]

Chorus Leader
Have you come with news of some fresh trouble
in our house of kings?

Messenger
          They're dead –
and those alive bear the responsibility.
We moved to the young girl's rocky cave,
the hollow cavern of that bride of death.
In the furthest corner of the tomb
we saw Antigone hanging by the neck,
held up in a noose – fine woven linen.
Haemon had his arms around her waist –
he was embracing her and crying out
in sorrow for the loss of his own bride,
now among the dead, his father's work.
Creon saw him, let out a fearful groan,
then went inside and called out anxiously,
'You unhappy boy, what have you done?
Come out, my child – I'm begging you – please come.'
But the boy just stared at him with savage eyes,
spat in his face and, without saying a word,
drew his two-edged sword. Creon moved away,
so the boy's blow failed to strike his father.
Angry at himself, the ill-fated lad
right then and there leaned into his own sword,
driving half the blade between his ribs.
While still conscious he embraced the girl
in his weak arms, and, as he breathed his last,
he coughed up streams of blood on her fair cheek.

Chorus Leader
Teiresias, how your words have proven true!

[*Enter* **Creon** *from the side, with attendants.* **Creon** *is holding the body of* **Haemon**]

Chorus Leader
Here comes the king in person – carrying
in his arms, if it's right to speak of this,
a clear reminder that this evil comes
not from some stranger, but his own mistakes.

Creon
Aaaii … My fear now makes me tremble.
Why won't someone now strike out at me,
pierce my heart with a double-bladed sword?
Alas for me … the guilt for all of this is mine –
it can never be removed from me or passed
to any other mortal man. I, and I alone …

Chorus
There's no release for mortal human beings,
not from events which destiny has set.

Creon
When such horrible things happen, heaven itself
seems to darken as if there are no gods, as if humans
dwell alone in a grey world without spirit.

Chorus
But to measure such horror, one needs gods.
The horror reaches well beyond the human scope.

Creon
Then take this foolish man away from here.
I killed you, my son, without intending to.
I don't know where to look or find support.
Everything I touch goes wrong, and on my head
fate climbs up with its overwhelming load.
If only events could be unwound
and take a different path, if I could reach back

and change my past decisions …

[*The attendants help* **Creon** *move up the stairs into the palace, taking Haemon's body with them. The* **Chorus** *remains on the scene; its leader repeats words already spoken, returning us to a previous moment*]

Chorus Leader
Go and release the girl from her rock tomb.
Then prepare a grave for that unburied corpse.
Go now and get this done. Don't give the work
to other men to do.

Creon
          I'll go just as I am.
Come, you servants, each and every one of you.
Come on. Bring axes with you. Go there quickly –
up to the higher ground. I've changed my mind.

Interlude – Chorus
There are many uncanny and demonic things,
but nothing more uncanny and demonic than man.
He's taught himself speech and wind-swift thought,
trained his feelings for communal civic life,
learning to escape the icy shafts of frost,
volleys of pelting rain in winter storms,
the harsh life lived under the open sky.
That's man – so resourceful in all he does.
There's no event his skill cannot confront –
other than death – that alone he cannot shun.
The qualities of his inventive skills
bring arts beyond his dreams and lead him on,
sometimes to evil and sometimes to good.
If he treats his country's laws with due respect
and honours justice by swearing on the gods,
he wins high honours in his city.
But when he grows bold and turns to evil,
then he has no city. A man like that –
let him not share my home or know my mind.
The most dangerous of these men – or women –

is the one who grows bold and turns to evil
in the way he obeys laws themselves.
Instead of controlling our demonic excesses,
laws become in his hands the tool of his demonic excess,
the ledge that he uses to sap the very foundations
of the city life. In an unnatural perversion, his evil
takes the shape of the ruthless will to enact justice.

[*A* **Messenger** *enters*]

Chorus Leader
Have you come with news of some fresh trouble
in our house of kings?

Messenger
                    They're dead –
and those alive bear the responsibility.
We moved to the young girl's rocky cave,
the hollow cavern of that bride of death.
In the furthest corner of the tomb
we saw Antigone in tears, while Haemon
had his arms around her waist. Led by Creon,
all three together went to the place
where Polyneices' corpse was left to be devoured by birds,
and performed a proper burial. But people who saw this
spread the rumour around the city, and the crowd
which considered Polyneices a traitor attacking his own city
was shocked and enraged. Passions flared up,
the crowd entered the royal palace, savagely slaughtered
Creon and Haemon, and, unable to restrain and control
their demonic passion, they went on a murderous spree
of destruction. Now the entire city of Thebes is on fire.

[**Antigone** *enters, dazed and half-crazy, she walks in a trance
among the ruins, with fires burning all around her*]

Antigone (*repeating*)
My nature is to love. I cannot hate …

Chorus
But the horror around you is nonetheless your deed.

Antigone
I am perplexed. How could all this destruction
be the outcome of my modest demand for a proper burial?
All I demanded was respect for our gods
and their immemorial laws …

Chorus
           Those in power
can afford to obey honour and rigid principles,
while ordinary people pay the price for it. Perhaps,
divine laws are not the ultimate authority. Perhaps,
something much more uncanny, a command much more weird,
lays dormant in the abyss of divine mystery. It is told
that Jews, a strange people that lives on the Eastern shore
of our great sea, sing an even stranger prayer
in the evening before their greatest holiday, Yom Kippur –
they call it Kol Nidre:

'All vows we are likely to make,
all oaths and pledges we are likely to take
between this Yom Kippur and the next Yom Kippur,
we publicly renounce. Let them all be relinquished
and abandoned, null and void, neither firm nor established.
Let our vows, pledges and oaths be considered
neither vows nor pledges nor oaths.'

There's a great wisdom in these words,
a wisdom that you ignored in your obstinacy.
A society is kept together by the bond of Word,
but the domain of logos, of what can be said,
always turns around a vortex of what cannot be said,
and this mysterious vortex is what all our endeavours
and struggles are about. Our true fidelity
is to what cannot be said, and the greatest wisdom
is to know when this very fidelity
compels us to break our word, even if this word
is the highest immemorial law. This is where
you went wrong, Antigone. In sacrificing everything
for your law, you lost this law itself.

Antigone

I just stood for justice, whatever the costs.
How can this be wrong?

Chorus

                    If your justice wins,
there will be no world in which its victory is to be seen.
We see how dedicated you are to your Cause,
ready to sacrifice everything for it. But wisdom tells us
that, sometimes, when you forsake everything for your Cause,
what you lose is the Cause itself, so all your sacrifices
were in vain, for nothing. Then you end up
not as a noble hero but as an abject
whose place is neither with the living nor with the dead,
but in the uncanny in-between where monsters abide
that our mind cannot even contemplate.

[**Antigone** *stands silent and motionless, with just a nervous
repulsive tic on her face*]

Antigone

Don't you realize that you're talking to a dead woman alive?

Chorus

It's because you run yourself out in a grief with no cure,
no time limit, no measure. It is a knot no one can untie.
Why are you so in love with things unbearable?

Antigone

By dread things I am compelled. I know that.
I see the trap closing. Now I know what I am.
But while life is in me I ask only one thing:
let me go mad in my own way. In this madness of mine
I will try to imagine how events could be unwound
even further back, to avoid this horror I'm in …

[**Creon** *reappears on the scene and we again return to a previous
moment*]

Chorus Leader

So she must die – that seems decided on.

Creon
Yes – for you and me the matter's closed.

Chorus
　　　　　But not for us,
the suffering people of Thebes. You pushed us too hard.
We are just tired of standing in the shadow, and allowed
to step forward just to comment your deeds, celebrating you
with empty wisdoms.

Creon
So you're taking that insolent girl's side?

Chorus
No, it's much worse for you. We now step forward
against both of you who, with your irresponsible conflict,
hold all of us as a hostage and threaten the survival
of the entire city. You're no longer fit to rule,
so we'll take over as a collective organ
and impose a new rule of law, deciding together.
Here is our first decision: Creon is no longer king,
he is deposed, both Creon and Antigone
are put under guard, and we proclaim ourselves
a people's court which will impose swift justice.
This matter cannot wait – our city has to start
breathing normally.

Creon
　　　　　But that's what I was doing.
I was just pragmatic for the good of the state …

Chorus
… and so are we, that's why we'll order you to be killed
as a punishment for your brutal acts.

Creon
　　　　　Yes, I was tough,
but as our common people say, no omelette can be made
without breaking some eggs …

Chorus
True, we see broken eggs
all around Thebes, but where is this omelette of yours?

Creon
Our troubles come from the horrible deeds
of Oedipus's breed. I just tried to control the damage,
as a master enforcing law and order
and limiting freedom when necessary. Let me repeat
the words I told you some time ago. We must obey
whatever man the city puts in charge,
no matter what the issue – great or small,
just or unjust. For there's no greater evil
than a lack of leadership …

Chorus
                    … here you are wrong.
Much greater evil than a lack of leadership
is an unjust leader who creates chaos in his city
by the very false order he tries to impose. Such an order
is the obscene travesty of the worst anarchy.
The people feel this and resist the leader. A true order,
on the contrary, creates the space of freedom
for all citizens. A really good master
doesn't just limit the freedom of his subjects,
he gives freedom. In our daily lives,
we are caught in our customs and cannot see beyond.
When you encounter a true master, he makes you aware
of things you didn't know you can do. His message is not
'You cannot!' or 'You have to…!', but 'You can!'
You can do the impossible, you can rebel. A true master
does not stand above us, people, he is a mediator
who vanishes while giving our freedom back to ourselves.

Creon
I see, I'm a dead man now, no way out. But let me just say …

Chorus
No! Guards, don't let him speak, kill him at once.
Take him into a dark corner of the palace

and dispose of him, then throw his corpse out
for scavengers to get, so that he will suffer
the same fate he ordained for Polyneices.

Creon
Why take me inside? If your deed is honourable,
what need of darkness?

Chorus
You shall not die on your own terms.

[**Guards** *take* **Creon** *away*]

Antigone
I hope I will be allowed this last honour.

Chorus
It remains to be seen …

Antigone
                    Why? Don't you see
I'm on your side? In demanding a proper burial for Polyneices,
I was giving voice to all those who are excluded,
without their own voice, leading a shadowy existence
at the margins of our city-state.

Chorus
But the excluded
don't need sympathy and compassion from the privileged,
they don't want others to speak for them,
they themselves should speak and articulate their plight.
So in speaking for them, you betrayed them even more
than your uncle – you deprived them of their voice.

Antigone
You perplex me with your sophistry. Whatever you insinuate,
I'm a good person, I can't be bought!

Chorus
The lightning which strikes the house,
also cannot be bought.

Antigone

      I hold to what I said.

Chorus

But what did you say?

Antigone

      I am honest, I say my opinion.

Chorus

Which opinion?

Antigone

      I am brave.

Chorus

      Against whom?

Antigone

I do not consider my personal advantages.

Chorus

Whose advantages do you consider then?

Antigone

Of the living and of the dead.

Chorus

But how does your consideration of the dead
help or hurt the living? Hear us then:
we know you are our enemy, an even more dangerous one
than your uncle. This is why we shall now
put you in front of a hole in the earth.
But in consideration of your merits and good qualities
we shall decapitate you with a good sword
and bury you with a good shovel in the good earth.

Antigone

No matter what you say, it's horrible
to kill a human being …

Chorus

      … but sometimes,
when doing nothing opens up a gate

to the flood of corpses, not to kill
can be an even greater crime.

Antigone

Is there

A choice in this for me?

Chorus

Of course there is.

You're free to choose your death.

Antigone

And if I don't?

Chorus
You will be put to death in any case.
But if you choose to freely meet your fate,
You die with dignity.

Haemon (*shattered*)
I see your reasoning,
sharp as a blade, but I remain divided
between your justice and my love for Antigone.
If I were perfect, I would offer myself
to swing the sword and punish her,
but I'm not strong enough to do it. Unable to decide
and choose, I prefer to end my life.

[*He draws a knife and cuts his throat. Members of* **Chorus**
simultaneously move towards **Antigone** *and strike her down with
swords*]

Chorus
There are many strange and wonderful things,
but nothing more strangely wonderful than man.
He's taught himself speech and wind-swift thought,
trained his feelings for communal civic life,
learning to escape the icy shafts of frost,
volleys of pelting rain in winter storms,
the harsh life lived under the open sky.
That's man – so resourceful in all he does.

There's no event his skill cannot confront –
other than death – that alone he cannot shun.
The qualities of his inventive skills
bring arts beyond his dreams and lead him on,
sometimes to evil and sometimes to good.
The most important part of true success
is therefore how to deal with man's demonic excess,
especially with the excess of those who rule us.
Since ruling over people strengthens this demonic excess,
no single man is fit to rule alone. It's only right
that they rule themselves collectively. In such a way,
they control each other to prevent demonic outbursts
which can lead to catastrophe. Even if there are no gods
to help them, such a collective of equals
is bound by a holy spirit, a bond stronger than fate,
a bond that can defy all earthly powers
and maybe even some divine.

Chorus Leader
Old wisdom has it right – we can't escape
the clutches of our fate. But what this wisdom
ignores is that we also can't escape the burden
of our responsibility. We cannot use our fate
as an excuse to do what pleases us.
The parents of Antigone's own father
knew in advance his fate and tried to avoid it,
but their very measures to achieve this noble end
helped the fate to realize itself. The bitter lesson
of Oedipus's story was that a man who has no choice
since evil is his fate, is no less fully guilty
for his disgusting deeds. But what Antigone's sad story
taught is that if we miraculously return in time
to change the course of the events that brought about
the present cataclysm, the new outcome
might even surpass the old one in horror and distress.

We've reached the end of Antigone's sad stories
– which of them is the one to follow?
Was she right in insisting to the end

on the respect for the divine unwritten laws?
Was Creon right in keeping in his sight
the common good of the city-state? Or was the Chorus right
in getting rid of both of them and in establishing
a common rule? There is no simple answer –
we, actors, are just shadows who deployed
the three diverging destinies to you, our spectators.
It's up to you to choose at your own risk and peril.
There is no one to help you here, you are alone.
When we're alone, when nothing happens, all of a sudden
we're hit by the murmur of life, and at that moment,
wise men know how to suspend the chaos and decide.

About the author

Slavoj Žižek is a Hegelian philosopher, a Lacanian psychoanalyst, and an engaged Communist whose vividly adventurous, unorthodox and wide-ranging writings have won him a unique place as one of the most high-profile thinkers of our time. He is a researcher at the School of Law, Birkbeck College, University of London, and Visiting Professor at the New York University, USA.

Also available from the same author

Disparities

The concept of disparity has long been a topic of obsession and argument for philosophers but Slavoj Žižek would argue that what disparity and negativity could mean, might mean and should mean for us and our lives has never been more hotly debated.

Disparities explores contemporary 'negative' philosophies, from Catherine Malabou's plasticity, Julia Kristeva's abjection and Robert Pippin's self-consciousness to the God of negative theology, new realisms and post-humanism, and draws a radical line under them. Instead of establishing a dialogue with these other ideas of disparity, Slavoj Žižek wants to establish a definite departure, a totally different idea of disparity based on an imaginative dialectical materialism. This notion of rupturing what has gone before is based on a provocative reading of how philosophers can, if they're honest, engage with each other. Slavoj Žižek borrows Alain Badiou's notion that a true idea is the one that divides. Radically departing from previous formulations of negativity and disparity, Žižek employs a new kind of negativity: namely positing that when a philosopher deals with another philosopher, his or her stance is never one of dialogue, but one of division, of drawing a line that separates truth from falsity.

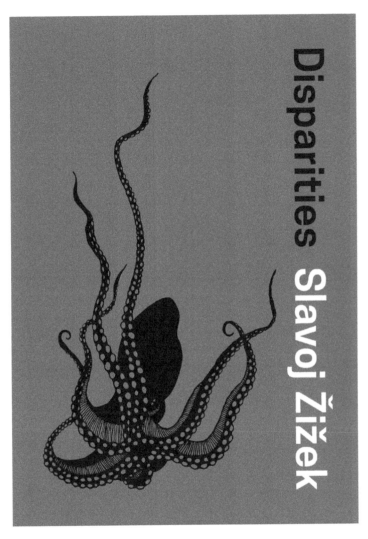

Disparities

Slavoj Žižek

Interrogating the Real

Covering psychoanalysis, philosophy and popular culture and drawing on a heady mix of Marxist politics, Hegelian dialectics and Lacanian psychoanalysis, the writings collected in *Interrogating the Real* reflect not only the remarkable extent of Slavoj Žižek's varied interests, but also reveal his controversial and dynamic style.

BLOOMSBURY
REVELATIONS

SLAVOJ ŽIŽEK

INTERROGATING
THE REAL

Edited by Rex Butler and
Scott Stephens

BLOOMSBURY

The Universal Exception

The Universal Exception brings together some of Slavoj Žižek's most vivid writings on politics. Combining high theory, popular culture and passionate engagement with politics, Žižek introduces startling new perspectives on such topics as multiculturalism, capitalism and Bill Gates, the revolutionary potential of Stalinism, the terrorist attacks of 9/11 and the war in Iraq.

Along with a glossary of key terms, the *Bloomsbury Revelations* edition also includes a new preface by the author.

SLAVOJ ŽIŽEK

THE UNIVERSAL EXCEPTION

BLOOMSBURY

www.ingramcontent.com/pod-product-compliance
Ingram Content Group UK Ltd.
Pitfield, Milton Keynes, MK11 3LW, UK
UKHW020706280225
455688UK00012B/297